This book is for
an incredible kid: you.

TATUM

(your name here)

★ ★ ★

Your future is your own;
make it everything you can.

Also by Ashley Rice

Girl Power
You Are a Girl Who Totally Rocks
You Go, Girl... Keep Dreaming

Library of Congress Catalog Card Number: 2008012668
ISBN: 978-1-59842-256-6

BLUE MOUNTAIN PRESS is registered in U.S. Patent and Trademark Office.
Certain trademarks are used under license.

Printed in China.
First Printing: 2009

Library of Congress Cataloging-in-Publication Data

Rice, Ashley.
For an incredible kid : —stories, tips, and advice about how to grow up strong / Ashley Rice.
    p. cm.
ISBN 978-1-59842-256-6 (trade pbk. : alk. paper) 1. Children—Life skills guides—Juvenile literature. 2. Teenagers—Life skills guides—Juvenile literature. I. Title.

HQ781.R515 2009
646.700835—dc22
                                                                          2008012668

Blue Mountain Arts, Inc.
P.O. Box 4549, Boulder, Colorado 80306

For an

Incredible
Kid

...stories, tips, and advice
about how to grow up strong

Ashley Rice

Blue Mountain Press™
Boulder, Colorado

Introduction

Life is full of brilliant moments, good days, and sunshine. It's also full of scraped knees and missed chances. But have you ever noticed that when you are having a scraped-knee kind of day, if you try talking to a friend, listening to your favorite CD, or even reading a good book, it can make you feel stronger? Sometimes you feel better knowing others go through the same things you do. Somehow good lyrics or a good story can turn what at first seemed to be disappointments into amazing experiences on the road of life — experiences that lead you to great things, teach you stuff, and make you an even more interesting person.

(By the way, you already are an interesting and amazing and incredible person.)

This book is filled with stories about growing up, which, like climbing mountains, can sometimes be tough and sometimes exhilarating. But that's the thing about challenges: you always walk away from them having learned something.

You are unique, it's true, and your life is not and never will be exactly like anyone else's (this is a good, miraculous, and even wonderful thing).

So whether you are dealing with the challenges of school and changing friendships, the different (and sometimes confusing) expectations of adults around you, or personal goals that aren't progressing the way you'd like them to, the first thing to do is to try not to worry too much! Some situations you may find yourself in CAN BE really tough, but you are stronger than anything you might come across. There is nothing you can't conquer — no matter what is going on around you — if you have the right mindset and believe in yourself.

Some ABCs for Growing Up

Act confident. Believe in yourself. Care about others. Dare to be different. Envision your dreams. Find something to love. Grant wishes. Hope hard. Invite possibility. Judge little. Keep promises. Laugh a lot. Make friends. Never give up. Open your mind. Plant miracle seeds. Question everything. Run as fast as you can just to see what it feels like. Stay true. Try whatever you can. Understand empathy. Volunteer. Win gracefully (when you win). X marks the spot to your dreams... (you'll get there). Yield to oncoming traffic. Zero in on what's important, and keep those things close to your heart — always.

The Cut

The Time I Didn't Make the Team

I have always wanted to be a runner. In fourth grade, the first year track was offered at my school, I tried out for the relay team.

Tryouts were held in the early mornings before school. Eliminations were made by having us race together in groups. We lined up at the starting line, ten girls at a time, to run the 100-yard dash.

The coach (one of my friends' dads) timed us. When all the groups had run, he called us back together. We already knew Lizzie would get the fastest time; long-legged with an older sister who ran marathons, she was an obvious athlete.

"Do you girls know who had the second fastest time?" the coach asked us dramatically. Next he said my name, which made me proud, but then to my horror he said, "So the rest of you must not be putting in much effort. Step it up, now! You can beat her." I immediately felt deflated.

We ran the same 100-yard dash three more times, and each time girls lined up on either side of me, determined to please our coach and run faster than I did. By the end of that first day I was eliminated.

I know it hurt not to have made the relay team that year, but so much has happened since then that I barely remember feeling sad. Long-distance track, which suited me better, was offered during middle school. By seventh grade my name was often announced over the loudspeakers as the winner of the one-mile run. In high school I was also a varsity team captain.

Rather than scaring me away from sports and other tryouts, the 100-yard dash lesson taught me something I would remember whenever anyone told me what I wanted to do was too difficult or that I did not have the potential. If you really want to pursue something you love, keep trying!

Stuff to Consider
When You're Trying Out
for the Team

1. The people who start out as the "very smartest," "very fastest," or "very" anything will not necessarily end up that way. Most things in life have less to do with "raw talent" than with putting your heart into everything you do, believing in yourself, and giving a sincere effort. In other words, you have as good a chance as anyone. Whatever you want to do, go for it.

2. Don't worry if you are not one of the coach's favorites or one of the teacher's pets. Just try to focus on your goals and do the best you can. Your teammates and peers will respect you for that.*

   *If you ARE a favorite or pet, that's great, too. Just remember that favoritism can be fickle and, just like luck, can change on a dime — so try not to depend on it.

A Friend Is...

A friend is a
laughter-filled day
to treasure when it rains.

A friend is
sunshine on an
otherwise gray day.

A friend is a
smile I will always
remember.

A friend is a
very special flower.

Messed-Up Scrapbook

Caught Between Two Friends

My friend Allie and I were hosting a scrapbook party at my place. I was busy getting supplies ready a few days before the party when I got a frantic phone call from her. She quickly explained to me that she had gotten into a fight with Cynthia — who was on our guest list — and went on to say that it would be impossible for her to be at the party with Cynthia. Allie asked me if I minded if we sent an e-mail to uninvite Cynthia.

I considered Allie's side of the story (and my own desire not to ruin a party we'd already planned) and then said, "Okay. Do whatever you need to do." I sincerely believed I could call Cynthia later on my own and explain to her that even though she was no longer invited to a party at my house, I did not hold anything against her and still wanted to be friends with her.

But how would I feel if I were suddenly uninvited from something, whatever the circumstances?

I thought about it some more and then called Allie back. "Why don't we just cancel the party? That way we won't hurt someone's feelings," I said. I told Allie she might even make up and become friends with Cynthia again over time (if she wanted to) but probably not if we uninvited her. Plus, we could always reschedule the party for later. After a pause, Allie said, "You know what? I think you're right."

Instead of sending a personal note to Cynthia, we sent a general note to everyone: "We're very, very sorry, but we will have to cancel the party this weekend. Please call if you want to get together." Friday night I hung out with Cynthia, and I spent Saturday with Allie. Even though we didn't get to make the scrapbooks, the spirit of friendship had been preserved.

Stuff to Consider
When Your Friends Are Fighting

1. Do not speak badly of one friend in front of the person with whom she is fighting and vice versa. You will only add fuel to the gossip fire, and if your two friends ever reconcile, you will possibly get burned yourself as a result of your words.

2. Friendships — like most things in life — can be bumpy and complicated. I can count my true friends on the fingers of one hand. I do not know what I would have done without them when I was growing up.

There will be good days
and bad days
in your life.
There will be times
when you want to laugh
and let it all out.
There will be times when
you want to shout out
in frustration.
But don't let the
"bad" days get you down.
Don't let your own
limitations or those of others
around you make you
frown.

Instead, accept your talents
as they are.
Grow each day a little more.
Learn as much as you can.
You will find that
"limitations" are only
guideposts that will point
you toward
an unexpected star.

Orange Teeth

Learning to Make Time for What Matters

I was seven, and I was eating tomato soup when my mom told me it was time to go to the dentist. She rushed me out the door and soon we were in the car, speeding down the road, me with orange teeth.

When I opened my mouth in the dentist's chair, he immediately asked me why I had not brushed my teeth after eating. I explained the time-constraint thing, but he wasn't buying it. "The first lesson you need to learn in life is that there is always time to brush your teeth," he said, stressing the word "always." And that was the end to our conversation.

As you get older, the orange-teeth situation may show up in your life in more complicated ways. Two of your teachers may schedule big tests on the same day that you have a book report or a job application due or lines to memorize for a school play. Sometimes you may have a test to study for on the same day that you have a big soccer game. Or maybe you're scheduled to babysit your little sister and also have to write a term paper.

Making good grades is a big part of steering yourself toward a good future. Some schools have rules that prohibit teachers from scheduling too many tests on the same day. If yours doesn't, you can try talking to one or more of your teachers and explaining your (and possibly also your classmates') predicament.

But as you get older, be prepared for an answer you may not like. In a writing class I took in college, I had a short story due on the same day that I had to turn in my thesis (a really long report that needs to be completed on time if you want to graduate).

"This story is not up to your usual standards," the teacher said to me. Though I had not been planning to mention anything, I blurted out to him that my thesis was due right after class.

There was a brief silence. "I don't care what else is going on in your life — if you have a thesis or a car payment or a baby due or you are DYING — when you come into this room, all that matters is the quality of your story."

On one level it was inspiring that the teacher was unyielding in his standards. But what I really learned from the ordeal was to plan WAY ahead, work VERY hard, and then do my best under whatever time constraints or circumstances I faced.

Stuff to Consider
When Your Schedule Gets Too Full

1. The best way to deal with not having enough time for everything you want to do is to prepare as far in advance as you can.

2. If you know when the tests and papers and athletic games and practices are going to be scheduled, mark them down on a calendar with different colored markers. You can even use stickers to make it fun. That way you can start studying or preparing your paper early and you won't be swamped and stressed out the night before.

Always do what you can...
to put a smile
on someone's face...
to be a friend to
someone who needs one.

Always do what you can...
to make the world
a better place
and to help someone else out
by being yourself.

Upside-Down Smile

Gossip Hurts

One day in January I received a group e-mail from Suzanne asking me to read her online diary.

Suzanne and I had been friends once but hardly ever saw each other anymore. We did different activities now, and in the past she hadn't been particularly nice to me or my friends whenever we met up to do something together.

In short, by that cold day in January when I received her group e-mail, we'd drifted far apart. As far as reading her every thought — it wasn't first on my list.

I saved the link to the diary and decided to read it later.

I remember the warm day in February when I did. Expecting to read about the musings or new happenings and interests of Suzanne, I instead found something completely different.

For whatever reason — maybe because we weren't really friends anymore — Suzanne had decided to use her new online diary mostly as a place to write a lot of mean things about me.

As I continued reading, confusion, anger, and a rainbow of other emotions raced through my head. I read about how, not long ago, Suzanne had gone to a place where I happened to be hanging out, too. When she saw that I was there, she snuck in and hid in the back to make sure I couldn't see her, and then she made sure to leave after I did. All this, according to her diary, was because she didn't want to have to say "hi" to me.

Temporarily disheartened, I deleted Suzanne's e-mail and shut down my computer. Then I went outside and rode my bike for a really long time.

Later, I sought out a friend who likes me for who I am to talk about what happened and help me get past my feelings of anger and sadness.

Even after you stop listening, gossip can still hurt.

Stuff to Consider
When Someone Gossips About You

1. You can't control other people's words or actions, so don't stress about that. You <u>can</u> control your own words and actions and use them in a positive way.

2. Never let anyone else's opinion define you. Ever. And pretty much everyone — from presidents to pop princesses — gets gossiped about sooner or later. Just remember: Gossip is like a monster that lives on your attention. The less attention you feed (pay) it, the sooner it will starve (go away).

3. Online diaries and blogs can be a fun way to express your creativity and keep in touch with friends by posting pictures, quotes, music, etc. If you write about people you know, think about what you say and why you are saying it.

You Are a Kid with a Lot of Heart

Life is as precious, fleeting, hopeful, challenging, and magical as the sweet music of a butterfly's two wings. With each step we grow up, and even as we fall, we grow strong.

The Leaves on the Trees

The Day I Got Eyeglasses

The first day of third grade, my teacher asked us to open our books to page seven, which I could read fine. But before the day was over, she put me in a different seat near the chalkboard because I had to squint to read the board from where I was sitting before. And even sitting up front, twice I had to ask the girl sitting next to me what it said.

That afternoon Ava, the school nurse, told me the headaches I'd been getting weren't because I was sick. My eyes were straining to see things far away, and I needed to get a pair of eyeglasses.

Later with my mom, I picked out small, silver-colored frames with a matching light-blue case.

Immediately I was startled by how detailed things looked when I had on my new glasses. The frames felt strange on my nose, especially the first time I wore them to school.

I wanted to take off my new glasses for recess, but I liked how they helped me see clearly. And the eye doctor said to wear them all the time except when I was going to bed. So I kept them on.

Near the side of the school I saw Robert, a kid from my class, swinging alone. Past him, I could see the individual leaves on the trees: a scene that would have been a blur to me before when I had thought all trees at a distance just looked green and fuzzy.

I was called into a pick-up game of kickball, but I felt off balance and was scared of the ball hitting me in the face. When I missed the ball, someone from the other team made a crack about my eyesight. Someone else joked about how nobody should pick me for a team again because of my new silver frames — words I might have brushed off on another day, but they caught me off-guard on my first day wearing glasses. I didn't say, "It's not like everybody has to be exactly the same." I didn't say, "It's not my fault I can't see things far away without glasses."

I picked up my backpack and silently went inside, leaving the game behind.

Then I heard a sound behind me.

Robert had followed me in. He looked at me like he had never seen me until then, which was funny to me because I was the one who got the glasses. He told me he was impressed I didn't tell on the bullies who were picking on me.

"You never tell on anybody," he blurted out. "I've never met anyone like that," he said, "ever."

So my first day of wearing glasses at school was not so bad after all. Someone had given me a compliment I wouldn't forget — and I could see the leaves on the trees.

Stuff to Consider
When You're Going Through a Change

1. If you are going through a change — whether it's getting glasses or being the tallest kid in class — you may find support in unexpected places, even from people who don't have the exact same issue to deal with. Parents and teachers can be good listeners and might have good ideas, too.

2. There may not always be someone right there to help you out, but don't worry about that. In the meantime you can find inspiration in movies, books, music, art, sports, or simply in the world around you.

3. If you are looking for information or inspiration for a situation or problem you are currently dealing with, visit your local library. Most public libraries not only have books and magazines but also movies and music you can rent for free with a library card.

In the Cafeteria

Rudeness... It Can Happen Anywhere

My first day of middle school, I stood at the front of the cafeteria, facing a sea of mostly unknown faces. I felt unsure of where to sit. Then I saw her: a girl I recognized from years earlier. Relief washed over me. I quickly walked to her table and placed my tray down next to hers.

"Um, that seat is saved," she said before rolling her eyes at her friend. My cheeks burned with embarrassment as I turned away and went to sit at a nearby table full of strangers.

Rudeness can happen on the playground, at the mall, or in the school cafeteria. I remember being nervous to enter the cafeteria if my best friends were not with me because I was terrified of making a mistake in where and with whom I chose to sit. I was scared that someone might be rude or mean to me, and I did not take chances or try to branch out socially. But years of experience have taught me differently.

Now I realize that many of my fears were probably unjustified and that in trying to protect myself from anyone and everyone I did not already know, all I really did was miss out.

Stuff to Consider
When Someone Is Rude to You

1. If someone is being rude to you for no reason, it is that person's problem. He or she could be trying to impress a certain clique, having a bad day, or experiencing a difficult time at home. Somebody else's insecurities have nothing to do with you, so try not to let another person stop you from reaching out and taking chances.

2. It's pretty much up to you when you should take a stand on a particular issue. If you or someone you know is treated unfairly or rudely because of gender, economic status, or race... if you feel that reacting will make a point and possibly change things in school or your town or government or even in your own or another person's life... then go for it. Kids have fought back and made a difference by giving school speeches, writing newspaper editorials and letters to elected officials, having car washes, bake sales, and yard sales, and collecting funds for (or even starting) charities. Doing something positive in response to something negative can make a very powerful statement.

Be true to yourself
because no one else
knows you like you do.
Be true to yourself
and always keep working
to make your dreams
come true.
Be true to your heart...
and to your mind
and to your soul...
and no matter where
you go...
there's no mountain
you can't climb.

You Are a Brave Person

Write down three times when you acted bravely:

1. _____
_____
_____
_____

2. _____
_____
_____
_____

3. _____
_____
_____
_____

Recital Blues

Surviving a Public Performance

During my first-grade piano recital I froze and completely forgot how to perform my piece, "Sunbird." I had been practicing at my teacher's house and at home for weeks, but when I got up on the stage in front of an audience, my hands just hovered motionless over the piano keys. While the audience sat there waiting, my mind raced but remained a total blank.

A few seconds later I still couldn't remember my recital piece, but I knew I needed to do something and quickly. I eked out a string of random chords (that did not go together well and were not part of any song). I played those chords again. Next, I stood up and curtsied (this was required by the teacher) as if I had really just played "Sunbird." I went backstage and acted like nothing was wrong.

The bad news was that my parents and my piano teacher — whom I eventually had to face — were disappointed and thought I wasn't living up to my potential. The good news was that by making it through a very challenging and embarrassing moment in front of my family and peers, I learned I could survive such a public moment, deal with it through improvisation, and move on.

Stuff to Consider
When You Have to Speak
or Perform in Public

1. When preparing for a performance of any kind, remember that there will be a live audience watching. Since I didn't practice in front of anyone other than my teacher and my family before the big day, I got extra nervous and forgot my recital piece.

2. Stage fright can hit at any time: when you're speaking in class, giving a presentation, or performing in sports events. You don't need to win an Academy Award for your book report or piano performance. But the best way to feel confident about yourself and what you're doing is to practice and then — whatever happens when you're up there — just give it your very best shot.

Caterpillar Days

Recognizing Jealousy

My friend Therese and I were sitting in our kindergarten classroom during free time when she pulled out my favorite book, <u>The Very Hungry Caterpillar</u>, and began to read the entire book aloud to me. I was astonished, as I could not read yet, and as far as I knew, neither could anyone else our age.

She carefully flipped through the pages, and as she read each page aloud, I heard the book's familiar phrases — but coming out of Therese's mouth — and my usual admiration for my friend soon combined itself with a brand-new emotion that I did not like but recognized instantly: jealousy. (Later it would be over Therese's perfect nose and feathery hair.)

But that night, I asked my dad to help me learn to read. He agreed. Within months I was reading on my own, and later in life I developed a real love for literature.

And as it turned out, my jealousy had been completely unfounded: Therese had simply memorized <u>The Very Hungry Caterpillar</u> to make me jealous.

Stuff to Consider
When You Are Feeling Jealous

1. Jealousy is the desire to be like someone else or to have what someone else has. Sometimes jealousy can fuel healthy competition; you may practice a lot harder if you want to become as good as one of your friends at a particular activity, such as a sport or musical instrument. But the green-eyed monster is usually just another case of the grass being greener on the other side. Whether it's your friend's naturally long legs or your brother's popularity you covet, worrying about why you don't have the same personality, body type, or niche in school as someone else won't get you anywhere.

2. There are two things that will allow you to make the greatest contribution to the world and that will make you happiest in the end:

   First... Stay true to yourself.

   Second... Always have the patience to achieve your goals and dreams.

I believe in happy ♡ days, sunshine, and dreams!

Speak Up

Finding My Own Voice

I was a pretty quiet person in elementary school, and my best friend, Allison, was a pretty loud person. We were always together since we liked to do a lot of the same stuff: ballet, sports, watching the same TV shows. And since she loved to talk and I didn't, I let her do a lot of the talking for me.

If we were in a group of kids waiting for the school doors to open in the morning and someone asked Allison and me whether we wanted to be in the game of Red Rover, I'd look at Allison, whisper my answer to her, and she'd tell the person who had asked, "Sure — absolutely. We'd love to."

"My best friend can't eat potatoes," Allison would tell her mom if I was eating dinner at her house so I wouldn't have to explain.

She and I were very close, like sisters. We had matching pajama tops. We memorized the names of the crayon colors and built elaborate mini-circus rides out of folded notebook paper on our desks.

If I wore a shirt to school that somebody didn't like, Allison would make them see how cool the shirt really was — even if it wasn't. I loved that someone like Allison could answer questions that were directed at me, because then I didn't have to say much. At that point in my life I was often afraid of saying the wrong thing.

Even though I sensed I probably needed to talk more if I wanted to speak well when I got older, "getting older" right then seemed a million miles away.

On the first day of school the following year, I was reading the list of students who would be in my class. I read to the very end, and Allison's name was not on the list. She had a different teacher.

My assigned seat in class was right up front, between a girl with a silver necklace and a boy who stuffed cheese up his nose to try to impress us whenever the teacher wasn't looking. I looked around and decided I could make friends and would try to speak up more. It would just be kind of hard at first because I'd been relying on the courage and words of my best friend, Allison.

Stuff to Consider
When You're Separated
from a Friend

1. Best friends stick up for each other all the time, and this is a great thing. Just make sure you also know how to stand on your own, too, because sooner or later there will be a time when you have to.

2. Don't worry if you are separated from someone you're friends with. Allison and I were friends for many years growing up — even after I learned how to make different friends.

 Seasons Change.

 Spring turns to fall.

 We write sometimes.

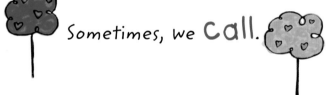 Sometimes, we call.

We face the days

 and through it all...

...friendship makes us strong.

Have a Nice Life

How to Say Goodbye

On the last day of school, I was waiting for a friend in a long hallway when a teacher who had never seemed to like me walked by. I was moving that summer, and I wouldn't be back to the school. I looked up and happened to catch the teacher's eye.

I should say something, I thought, but... what?

"Have a nice life," the teacher said to me sarcastically and then turned and disappeared down the hall.

Though caught off-guard, I realized by the way his words made me feel that what he had said was rude. I decided I would never say those words.

A few years later I was at another school "checking out" with the school's main office.

Selma, the woman behind the front desk, was in charge of school attendance and other things like that and always grinned at everyone. "See you next year," she said to me when my turn was over. "You have yourself a great summer, Kiddo."

And though I probably could have just said, "Okay," I told her, "I just graduated."

"Oh!" she said, surprised, double-checking my record. "Well... then you have a nice life," she said sincerely.

Outside in the car, I still didn't know for sure where I would be "tomorrow," but I realized that saying goodbye didn't have to be a bad experience. And it didn't matter that much what words you used to say it. What mattered was how you said it.

Stuff to Consider
When Saying Goodbye

1. Humor can get you through a million different stressful situations: it puts life into perspective, which makes just about anything feel a lot easier to deal with... even during happy, sad, or unexpected changes in your life.

2. Some goodbyes are permanent, some are temporary, and sometimes it's hard to tell the difference. Try to leave each place on a good note if you can.

3. If you are leaving somewhere like summer camp or a faraway relative's house, you can write letters and send jokes, photos, and stories about your life until you see your friends or relatives again.

Special Flowers

Remembering My Grandmother

My grandmother loved flowers, my grandfather, and telling stories about how high school was in the olden days.

Though we did not live near each other, when I got a little older, I would occasionally make the drive to her farm. We would look through old photographs, most of which were not labeled with names or dates. I would ask her who the people in the pictures were and what they did. I heard amazing stories about barn raisings and milk trucks and square dances. I heard a lot about the past and my family's history.

When she died, there was a trunk full of old photographs we hadn't gotten around to looking at. My grandmother would have known each name, face, and place. Since my grandfather is blind, he couldn't tell me who was in these pictures, but I knew that in his mind he could still see the long-ago moments the photos captured.

My grandmother's flowers continue to spring up around her old farmhouse, and there are many days when I miss her. When that happens, I remember her laugh or her love of telling me all those stories. And then, knowing that life goes on in the face of everything constantly changing around me, somehow I know that I can face my own future.

Stuff to Consider
When You Lose Someone You Love

1. When someone dies — whether you knew them well or their passing left only a small vacancy in your life — it is important that you grieve for them in your own way. Some people may turn to prayer. Others may visit their loved one's gravesite, bringing flowers, letters, or gifts. Some people simply keep those who've passed on in their thoughts and hearts.

2. Identify what you learned from the person and take that special knowledge — that gift — with you as you grow up and go on with your life. That is the very best gift you could ever give them.

When somebody dies, a cloud turns into an angel and flies up to tell God to put another flower on a pillow. A bird gives the message back to the world and sings a silent prayer that makes the rain cry. People disappear, but they never really go away. The spirits up there put the sun to bed, wake up the grass, and spin the earth in dizzy circles. Sometimes you can see them dancing in a cloud during the daytime when they're supposed to be sleeping. They paint the rainbows and also the sunsets and make waves splash and tug at the tide. They toss shooting stars and listen to wishes. And when they sing wind songs, they whisper to us, "Don't miss me too much. The view is nice, and I'm doing just fine."

On Having the Courage to Ask for Help

As you get older, facing up to the consequences of your actions is a big part of growing up. If you make a mistake, don't be afraid to tell someone or to ask for help or advice. This is the best way to learn from your actions...

...and keep on growing up strong.

Members Only

The Time I Overcommitted

One year I became secretary of a busy club at my school.

The secretary was responsible for, among other things, writing and sending out thank-you notes to people who helped us with school events.

Though I really wanted to be a member of the club because it was fun, I was busy that year and hadn't wanted the secretary position or any leadership position at all. But everyone around me grinned when my name was called, and I didn't know how to say "No" to a responsibility I considered to be a huge compliment. So instead of being realistic and admitting I probably had too many other responsibilities in my life to do a good job, I simply grinned back.

I thought I could just make time to complete all the secretary's responsibilities. A few months passed and I scraped by with doing my duties — just barely.

Then one day in November I was walking toward the gym when someone stopped me. It was Eleanor, the club's president.

"I thought you told me you sent that thank-you note to Peter Arlington," she said, not as a question. "Peter's my friend, and he said he didn't receive any thank-you note from our club."

She was right. I had looked up Peter's address in a book of addresses we had at school, but it wasn't listed there, and I was never able to find it. I had put it in the back of my mind to do later. Then I got busy and forgot.

I told all this to Eleanor, knowing it wouldn't help the situation. "I'm sorry," I said, embarrassed.

At that point, though I was still in the club, I had lost the trust of Eleanor and a few other people, too.

Now I really wished I'd asked someone in the club to help me out or I'd been realistic to begin with. I should have told them to give the position to someone else who would have had time to do a better job.

Stuff to Consider
When You Take on Too Much

1. I did the wrong thing in this story: I overcommitted myself because at the time saying "Yes" felt a lot easier than saying "No." Later the consequences caught up with me.

2. If you are always trying to please others without considering your own feelings — or busy schedule — many times you'll just end up frustrating yourself and all the people counting on you. On the flip side, if you are honest with yourself and others, you'll be more likely to earn the respect of those around you.

On Growing Up and Being Yourself

Don't let other people's ideas about things over-influence you. Listen to criticism and learn from it, but take it with a grain of salt. Only you really know what you are capable of doing. Sometimes people will judge you on how good you are at something right now and fail to consider your to ability to learn and grow.

High-Five

The Day I Learned
My Best Was Good Enough

There are the best and bravest athletes, and then there are the athletes who are pretty good, which was me.

I was pretty good at lots of things: doing gymnastics in friends' front yards, running races, playing tag, roller-skating, and swimming. I was <u>not</u> good at teamwork or being aggressive — and especially not at the same time — so my very worst sport was soccer.

Soccer practice was three times a week. My mom and my friends' moms carpooled us all in one car, which was great. Soccer practice meant lots of fun things to me like dribbling the soccer ball around orange cones and running laps around the trees in the park. But when it came to playing games against teams from different schools on Saturday mornings, the fun was pretty much gone for me because I became a nervous wreck. I did not quit because most of the time soccer was fun. We won some, we lost some — pretty much like most of the other teams, I figured.

Then somehow our team was selected to play in the "Under the Lights" game, where teams are placed in a large local football stadium with enormous lights shining down on the field. The referee blew the whistle, and our game began.

I guess a lot of people on both teams were confused by how bright everything was — or maybe by the sensation of having so many different people in the bleachers looking down on them and watching their every move. Sometime during the second quarter I was playing right wing (my favorite position, but one I rarely played as right wing was normally reserved for real athletes). Since it was a special occasion, the coach had let us pick whatever position we wanted.

I saw the ball ahead of me and ran for it, and nobody tried to stop me. I ran and I ran, heading for the net where the goalie was. I kicked that ball as hard as I could with my right foot. And then, with the bright lights shining down on the field, I made my first game goal ever.

We went back to our positions, and a few minutes later, the exact same thing happened again. I could not believe it! By the end of the game, I had made three game goals for the first time in my life. Everyone said "Congratulations!" and kept giving me high-fives and large grins. It was kind of like when we said "Good game, good game" to every player on the opposing team while slapping hands with them at the end of a game, but even more special.

I was not really good at soccer. I never would be good at it again. But I never stopped playing.

Stuff to Consider
When You're Not Great at Something

1. Doing something that might not be your VERY BEST or MOST favorite sport, art form, or activity can teach you fun things and lead you to good times, good friends, skills, thrills, and unexpected moments.

2. No matter how old you get, you will never, ever forget an experience like that "Under the Lights" game. For a few minutes (which seemed like forever) I felt like a star. (And this is coming from a girl who showed up on game days mostly so as not to miss out on the free can of soda awarded to each player at the end of a game.)

What Is Success?

Success is standing on your own two feet. Success is knowing you've done your best. Success is giving it your best shot. ☺ ☺ Success is telling the people you care about that you do. Success is staying encouraged in the face of life's obstacles and picking yourself up when you fall. Success is being yourself. Success is learning something new every day.

Fun Lists to Keep in Your Back Pocket or in the Pocket of Your Backpack

---

List #1
Cool Ways to Get Through a Bad Day

1. Take a walk, ride your bike, skateboard, walk your dog, or in-line skate to clear your head.

2. Go outside, lie down on your back on the grass, and look up at the sky. If this is not possible, lie down on your back on the carpet in your room. This activity may sound strange, but it really works. Feeling the force of gravity causes your body to relax, your problems to seem smaller, and you to feel grounded. Plus, it only takes a few minutes.

3. Create a poem, write in your journal, or blog about your life — you may find out things about yourself that you didn't even know you were thinking.

4. Send cards or e-mails to your friends.

List #2
How to Deal with Almost Anything

1. If you are disappointed in yourself, immediately think of a plan of action for how you can start improving.

2. The best defense against nervousness is to be thoroughly prepared. Don't forget to practice whatever it is you want to do!

3. Stare down your deepest fears and turn them into things you can overcome or accomplish.

4. Look for heroes, good days, and possibilities.

List #3
You Have the Power to Make Real Miracles Happen

1. Give your word — and then stick to it.

2. Lend your heart and hands to someone who needs them.

3. If you make a mistake, own up to it and try to fix what you did. If you don't know how, find someone who can help.

4. Be a good friend.

5. Find your own story, your own song, your own way of looking at things.

6. Give and accept compliments.

7. Work toward your dreams every day.

8. Live your life with all your heart.

You Are an Incredible Kid

Words to Help You
Grow Up Strong

As you go on in this world, always believe in your dreams. Keep looking forward to the future... to all you might be. Don't let old mistakes or misfortunes hold you down: learn from them, forgive yourself... or others... and move on. Do not be bothered or discouraged by adversity. Instead, meet it as a challenge. Be empowered by the courage it takes you to overcome obstacles. Learn something new every day. Be interested in others and what they might teach you, but do not look for yourself in other people's approval. As far as who you are and who you will become...

...the answer is always within yourself. Believe in yourself. Follow your heart and your dreams. You... like everyone... will make mistakes. But so long as you are true to the strength within your own

heart... you can never go wrong.